Bathrooms

Bathrooms

Ellen Stamper

HEARST BOOKS

A Division of Sterling Publishing Co., Inc.

New York

A Primrose Production
Designed by Niloo Tehranchi

Library of Congress Cataloging-in-Publication Data
Stamper, Ellen.
  Country living bathrooms / by Ellen Stamper.
      p. cm. -- (Easy transformations)
  ISBN 1-58816-286-9
    1. Bathrooms. 2. Interior decoration. I. Title: Bathrooms.
II.Country living (New York, N.Y.) III. Title. IV. Series.
  NK2117.B33S73 2003
  747.7'8--dc21
2003006324

10 9 8 7 6 5 4 3 2 1

Published by Hearst Books
A Division of Sterling Publishing Company, Inc.
387 Park Avenue South, New York, NY 10016

www.countryliving.com

Distributed in Canada by Sterling Publishing
c/o Canadian Manda Group, One Atlantic Avenue, Suite 105
Toronto, Ontario, Canada M6K 3E7

Distributed in Australia by Capricorn Link (Australia) Pty. Ltd.
P.O. Box 704, Windsor, NSW 2756 Australia

Manufactured in China

ISBN 1-58816-286-9

Contents

Foreword

Whether you are lucky enough to have a private bathroom as an extension of a master bedroom suite or a single room shared by the entire household, the bathroom is one place where convenience, style and comfort are of the utmost importance.

Throughout this book, you'll see some wonderful examples with inspirational ideas and valuable tips on transforming your own bath. You'll also realize how adaptable today's country style is for this special room of the house, regardless of whether you live in a modern city apartment or an older, period style home. There are simple ideas to give a fresh new look to an existing bath, tips on retrofitting an outdated design, and points to consider if you're lucky enough to be building the home of your dreams.

While budget will always be a consideration, not every bathroom makeover has to be costly. Country style is all about mixing old and new— working with the things you have before shopping for the things you want. There are simple ways to transform any bath. Consider giving yours a face-lift with a new coat of paint or wallpaper treatment. New towels, a shower curtain and bath mat are also great ways to add design, color and tex-ture to your bath. For a distinctive touch of country, think about replacing a standard medicine cabinet with one that has a vintage pine frame or use a milk glass candy dish (perhaps one you bought for $1.00 at your neighbors garage sale) as a decorative soap caddy.

Bathroom storage is usually at a premium; glass and metal canisters, baskets, wall-mounted shelves, and antique and vintage-styled armoires offer practical solutions with decorative benefits.

If your bathroom is in need of more than just a quick fix, you will find plenty of ideas and pointers in the pages that follow, from advice on replacement fixtures to the luxury touches that can transform a bath into a personal spa retreat. There's also advice on when to consider the services of a professional architect, certified bath designer or contractor.

Whether you're considering a simple makeover or a major transformation, this book was meant for you. Let it be your inspiration and guide in realizing your own dream bath.

Nancy Mernit Soriano,
Editor-in-Chief, *Country Living*

Introduction

During the last century, the lowly bathroom made a major transformation from utilitarian afterthought to treasured oasis. What was once quite literally an add-on room to an existing house is now an integral part of the initial planning of many new homes. It was inevitable that once bathrooms came indoors people would begin refining them to make them more practical and functional. No longer is it necessary to wall off a portion of some room in order to squeeze three relatively large pieces of porcelain into some semblance of organization.

Many of us do not have the luxury of designing a bathroom from the ground up; but that does not mean that we cannot have a space that fits our needs. This is one of the most wonderful features of country style. It is versatile and forgiving in ways that many other styles are not.

Country style means different things to different people. From the warm, rich colors and delightful toile prints of French Country to the charming mix of patterns that characterize English Country to our own homegrown use of natural materials, the various interpretations of country may look different on the outside—

but on the inside, they have much in common. This particular style always comes from the heart and is based on our human desire for warmth, comfort, and informality. It is a style that is organic, natural, and never over-thought. It is also a style that lends itself to constant change: perhaps it starts with existing fixtures, then adds a handcrafted art piece, followed by upgraded fixtures. Or maybe it's a room full of found objects. Whatever their origin, strangers, whether they be objects or humans, are always welcome.

Because of its innate flexibility, a room in the country style may be refreshed, updated, or thoroughly altered quite easily. There are many reasons for making a change in your bathroom. Perhaps you have young children (or frequent visits from grandchildren), in which case you'll need to think about child safety. You'll also want to think about the ease of using the various facilities with a small child. Another concern is creating a bathroom design that is flexible enough to grow with your family.

Other family considerations include accommodating older family members or those with physical challenges. Fortunately, the concept of universal design has given us many new and sensible choices for making the bathroom practical for all occupants. The wonderful thing about universal design is that it works well and makes sense for everyone, so its principles can be incorporated into any bathroom.

Perhaps your needs aren't as overt as an expanding or changing family. Perhaps it's simply that your fixtures are old or worn out. Or maybe you just feel you need a change. Whatever your motivation, there are so many options available that you can make a noticeable change whatever your budget.

This book is designed to assist you in making change easier. Each chapter reflects specific bathroom problems and design challenges. Whether you are working with a small space, inherited fixtures, or just want to introduce some color, you will find many creative options from which to choose. You will also see dream bathrooms as well as more modest spaces. Use this book as an idea bank, a design resource, or a creative inspiration. You may feel that not every idea is right for you. That's just fine. Or maybe you like a particular room but feel that

it would look better in a warmer or more vibrant color. Whatever the case, the examples and suggestions here are a jumping off point on the way to the bathroom of your dreams.

Sensible Bathroom Design

With all of this in mind, the first question to ask is how to begin. If you start with a plan, the project will seem much less overwhelming. First, imagine your dream space... Is it a master bathroom? A family bathroom? A powder room? Or perhaps a home spa? Then ask yourself: is this a renovation or a remodeling job? Think about what the room will require in terms of structural changes, tangible additions, and cosmetic enhancements. Take stock of what you already have. Make a realistic assessment of the size of the space; then define your needs very specifically. Be sure to note which items are necessities versus which are wants.

Once you've clarified your vision in your own mind, consider your budget: how much money do you really have—relocating plumbing or electrical lines are not weekend projects and will require the services of professionals.

Now begin your research to get a ballpark sense of what materials, fixtures, and labor cost. Remember that labor is a big part of any budget, generally around 21 percent. Items like cabinetry and fixtures/fittings typically weigh in at around 33 percent and 16 percent, respectively. You will have to work back and forth with your initial budget and your ballpark figures, making choices about where to compromise with regard to quality of materials. Home improvement experts also advise that it is not unusual for these projects to run up to 20 percent over budget, so make sure to include this in your final figures. It's much better to know ahead of time what the real cost of renovation will be so you can scale back before it's too late.

You can of course save a lot by doing much of the labor yourself but unless you are—or want to be—a dedicated do-it-yourselfer, this can be a time-consuming process. Think carefully about whether you have the time and energy to devote to doing the project yourself. It's especially important to look at this issue realistically if you already have a full-time job.

Should you decide to have professionals handle the whole project from start to finish, you'll need to decide which type of specialist is right for your job:

Architects are professionals with degrees in architecture and who carry state licenses. They're the proper choice when making structural changes because they're qualified to create structurally sound designs that are also attractive and functional. Architects can take your project from start to finish, overseeing the work of other experts. Some are members of the American Institute of Architects (AIA).

Bathroom Designers are planners with expertise in the latest furniture and fixture trends though they may not have the structural knowledge of architects or the aesthetic sense of interior designers. Look for bathroom designers who are members of the National Kitchen & Bath Association (NKBA) or a Certified Bathroom Designer (CBD), a specialist certified by the NKBA.

Interior Designers can supplement the work of architects and bathroom designers when it comes to the final aesthetic touches that complete a room. They also have access to materials and products not normally available to the general public through standard retail channels. Many interior designers belong to the American Society of Interior Designers (ASID).

General Contractors handle construction though some may also have design expertise.

They either do all the work themselves or hire subcontractors for various parts, order materials, and manage the completion of the job. Contractors also arrange for necessary permits and inspections.

With regard to selecting the various professionals to work on your bathroom, it's very important to do your homework. Ask people you know who have had work done on their bathrooms. Ask whether they were satisfied with the work. When calling professionals, don't be afraid to ask them for references. Then follow up with those references to make sure that the clients were satisfied with the work. Get more than one estimate. Don't make your final choice based on price alone because an inexpensive job that is poorly done will only cost you more in the long run.

RIGHT: Clean lines help marry the Asian style of the benches with the classic styling of the mirror and contemporary styling of the sink.

White on White

The all-white bathroom has gotten a bad reputation. Often considered boring, this classic look is anything but. White can give your bathroom a timeless quality if utilized properly because it works with any style and texture. It is extremely versatile and a great way to maximize your budget whether you are planning a complete bathroom redo or just want to freshen the room with a mini-makeover. There are two key issues to think about when working in white: Tonality and texture. Consider the shade of white—this will determine the mood—that you will use. So you want cool, blue undertones? Or perhaps warmer, with hints of apricot? Texture is what will add visual interest to the room.

RIGHT: This breathtaking example of a monochromatic theme hits all the right...or should we say white...notes. Clean lines give a timeless quality. Ample use of different textures including molding, marble, and glass adds depth and visual interest. Light-reflecting elements like the glossy paint finish, glass doors, and nickel hardware make the room come to life.

VARYING THE SIZE AND SETTING OF MARBLE TILES CREATES TEXTURE AND IS VISUALLY MORE EXCITING THAN A SINGLE SLAB OF MARBLE.

OPPOSITE: This simple little bath has the feel of a small luxury hotel. Though none of the individual elements are particularly expensive, they are carefully chosen to add up to a clean, fresh, soothing look. The small vase of flowers and unwrapped soaps add a refined touch.

LEFT: The use of under-mounted sinks allows for a clean, unbroken line in the marble slab top of the wash-stand, creating a generous display space for commonly used items. The lack of a top-mounted edge keeps the space from feeling cluttered, even with several objects present.

TRIMMING THE MEDICINE CHEST IN MOLDING HELPS TO INTEGRATE IT INTO THE REST OF THE ROOM'S ARCHITECTURE.

Keep It Interesting

- Incorporate texture
- Mix paint finishes (flat, satin, gloss)
- Add fabric
- Use faux or distressed finishes if natural materials don't fit your budget
- Use more than one shade of white

AN ÉTAGÈRE IS A PER-
FECT STORAGE PIECE
WHEN YOU HAVE
ATTRACTIVE OBJECTS
LIKE THESE VINTAGE
TOWELS TO DISPLAY.

ABOVE: Elegant vintage details create a lovely feminine ambience in this shabby-chic style bathroom. Each piece is gently worn— nothing feels too new—in a way that is consistent throughout the room. The period sink and mirror flanked by the vintage sconces form a focal point; the room needs no other ornamentation.

RIGHT: Sun pouring in through the windowed door warms this white space, giving it a soft, creamy glow. Light can be a wonderful ally when decorating with white. The pristine condition of each piece clearly illustrates that vintage-style chic doesn't have to be shabby.

L E F T : Nature becomes the star in this bathroom.
Tiling and fixtures are deliberately simple so that
expansive windows can frame the main attraction:
a spectacular natural vista.

A B O V E : The "when life gives you lemons…"
approach in this bathroom really pays off with the
dramatic impact that this boulder makes as the centerpiece of the room. Its sculptural presence
is enhanced by the tranquil all-white space.

RIGHT: Whites don't need to be identical in order to work well together. The different shades of white on the fixtures and upper wall are a welcome contrast to the softer white of the tiles. The texture of the wall tiles and beaded board door create another level of visual interest. Use of a dark wood floor is one way to ground the room.

OPPOSITE: The slightly faded gentility of this room is a perfect approach when working with worn fixtures. The key is making the "wear" seem deliberate by incorporating it consistently throughout the room. Note the distress on the mirror, tub, cabinet, and table. Set against the creamy white walls, the fixtures have a calming, soothing effect.

WHITE IS A PERFECT BACKDROP FOR ART; HERE, THE PAINTING FUNCTIONS ALMOST AS A WINDOW.

Vintage Chic

Vintage is the essence of country style. It shows an appreciation of the past, and is an ideal solution if you inherit older fixtures. But vintage doesn't necessarily imply a single period or style. Instead it is an unrestricted aesthetic that can be used to encompass any period that is not the present. There are some wonderful ways to freshen up older fixtures to give them a timeless chic without ripping out the whole bathroom. You can also introduce salvaged pieces into a new bathroom. Vintage and new can be mixed in various ways to create a flavor of times past without overwhelming the room.

RIGHT: This authentic Victorian bath has a decidedly masculine feel. The deep, mahogany-stained walnut wood sets the tone for the room. The color is then repeated in the reproduction floor tile and wallpaper. A rich mixture of several ornate patterns in the wall coverings, floor tile, shower stall, and stool fabric are typical of Victorian-era decor.

THE MODERN TUB DESIGN IS CAMOUFLAGED BY THE FURNITURE-LIKE WOOD ENCLOSURE.

OPPOSITE: Inherited fixtures can form the focal point in a bathroom but that doesn't mean the room has to be a museum. The clawfoot tub and marble sink are authentic to this early nineteenth-century home, but the room has a timeless feel because the original waist-high wainscoting has been extended to create a more visually interesting line that draws the eye upward. The updated color palette lends the room a fresh, open quality not typically found in authentic Victorian style.

LEFT: Vintage is often about finding new or different uses for old objects. This sink has been fashioned from a 200-year-old Chinese frying pan, giving it the look of a rustic fountain.

THE LIGHT FIXTURE IS MOUNTED IN A ROUGH TIMBER BEAM.

ABOVE: Antique stores are a great place to start when it comes to sourcing vintage items. The designers of this bathroom found all of the furnishings, including the fixtures, Amish cupboard, sconces, and freestanding mirror in this bathroom at antique stores.

RIGHT: Older fixtures like these are quite common in many homes but they have been rejuvenated here in several ways. The 1940s tub has been re-enameled; the sink sports a piped, pleated skirt; and the shower received a matching piped pelmet. Carrying the greens and yellows around the room helps visually tie the bathroom into the adjoining bedroom. Because the room is so tiny and the color palette so bold, small spots of color dotted throughout the room make a big impact without overwhelming the space.

ABOVE: Vintage tile is a great way to recreate an authentic feel in a room. This vintage 1927 Arts and Crafts bathroom features Batchelder tiles, known for their matte glazes and intricate detailing.

RIGHT: Victorian is a popular vintage style but not everyone wants the ornate, cluttered feel of that era. In this cottage-y modern approach, Victorian elements are paired with clean, simple lines and minimal color. Vintage style lighting fixtures, as well as a classic lion's paw tub and graceful double basin sink with authentic hardware, anchor the room. The use of beaded board paneling on the walls and ceiling creates texture but its clean lines don't look cluttered or fussy. The chair is a nice vintage addition, but again the lines keep the feeling more cottage-style than cluttered.

Vintage Sources

- Salvage yards
- Flea markets
- Auctions
- Estate sales
- Antique shops
- Resale shops

- Yard sales
- Online vintage supply houses
- Fixture suppliers that create reproduction fixtures

THE CEILING HAS BEEN PAINTED TO TIE IT INTO THE ROOM'S DESIGN.

LEFT: The inventive new uses for odd items give this bathroom a one-of-a-kind charm. Different textures, eras, and styles are juxtaposed to dramatic effect. The screen, fashioned from old French doors, makes a unique privacy shelter for the tub without the obstruction of a permanent wall. The wrought iron chair is actually a piece of garden furniture. Classic, though somewhat casual, beaded board is paired with the more elegant striped wall covering above it. The whole look comes together because the clean lines and relative simplicity of both background treatments allow the more ornate aged pieces like the sink and screen to take a starring role.

LEFT: Old gutter pipes get a new lease on life as legs for the elegant 1920s marble sink. The tin-paneled mirror in its original oxidized frame provides a balancing element to counteract the heavy sink legs.

ABOVE: These older bathroom fixtures were rejuvenated when the walls and built-ins were sheathed in a coat of fresh white paint. The thin strip of green wall tile and matching floor offer a soothing contrast.

Soothing Spaces

A home spa is the ultimate luxury in modern bathroom design. This once-humble room has become a quiet, peaceful refuge from the cares of the outside world. In recent years, manufacturers have risen to the challenge by creating beautiful home bath fixtures with all the conveniences of their commercial spa counterparts. There are choices available to suit almost any space, design style, or budget. The key to creating a personal retreat is focusing on colors, textures, and materials that are soothing and relaxing to you because it's all about creating a mood that calms.

RIGHT: This glorious garden bathroom is a mixture of vintage, cottage style, and modern elements, all tied together with the soothing neutral gray and white color palette. The generously sized whirlpool tub accommodates two and serves as the focal point of the room. Two sets of double French doors leading to the garden bring in plenty of light and add to the charm and character of the room.

A CANDLELIT CHANDELIER CREATES A RELAXING AMBIANCE.

LEFT: Sunlight floods through these large windows, making this magnificent space feel as if it were one with the outdoors. Warm blond wood tones on the floor and vanity echo the effect of the natural sunlight. An additional small window above the tub offers the bather a discreet view of the surrounding countryside.

THESE CUBBIES MAKE GOOD USE OF WHAT WOULD OTHERWISE BE WASTED SPACE UNDER THE INSET WINDOWS.

ABOVE: The modern take on a vintage style tub anchors this clean and soothing garden bathroom. The beaded board vanity keeps the feeling casual. The sheer spaciousness and high, raftered ceiling of the room give that airy, spa-like quality that allows the rest of the decor to remain minimal.

ABOVE: A large whirlpool tub nestled in a bay
window is a luxurious place to soak your cares away.
Sheer curtains add privacy but allow a generous
amount of light into the room. The large tub surround
provides a convenient place to rest a cup of tea or
keep towels close at hand.

AN UPHOLSTERED CHAIR
LENDS AN UNEXPECTEDLY
SOFT TOUCH TO THE ROOM.

RIGHT: Classic lines help integrate the various elements in this tranquil Victorian-style master bath. Marble surfaces create an instant sense of luxury.

OPPOSITE: Architectural columns form the framework of the shower and shelves, creating a smooth transition between the two. A soaking tub and a generously sized shower are true luxuries. With the pedestal base, this modern spin on the classic Victorian tub could still blend successfully into either a contemporary or vintage setting.

A TOWEL BAR ON THE TUB KEEPS TOWELS NEARBY.

L E F T : The warm European elegance of this classic bathroom comes from a combination of colors, textures, and materials. Attractive his-and-hers vanities flank the freestanding tub, but opulent fixtures tell only part of the story. The deep wall color serves as a warm neutral background against which the other layers are built.

A B O V E : Golden tones in the composite quartz surfaces surrounding the tub, vanity, and the shower wall echo the tones of the wall color. Brass hardware on the sink, tub, towel bars, and vanity hardware reinforces the warmth of the color scheme.

Create a Home Spa Atmosphere

- Choose soft colors and textures
- Install a rain-style or massaging showerhead
- Look for an extra-depth bathtub
- Opt for a tub instead of a shower
- Include a whirlpool
- Locate the tub near a window
- Upgrade to plush towels
- Store common bath items in attractive baskets
- Fill the room with scent
- Bring the outdoors in with plants and flowers

ABOVE: Sometimes a soothing place is anywhere that you can close the door and have a few moments' peace. This room is a great example of a small, private refuge. It's all about the attitude. The deep vintage tub is great for soaking. The overall effect is simple and pretty...both of which are qualities that are achievable on a limited budget.

RIGHT: Even if you don't have a flowerbed outside your bathroom, you can still recreate the aura of one. Abundant plants lend this room a garden atmosphere. Soothing neutral colors and a high, vaulted ceiling reinforce the outdoorsy atmosphere by enhancing the sense of space and airiness. The decorated panel surrounding the mirror makes it a part of the window architecture.

Small Space Solutions

A small bathroom doesn't have to be a big inconvenience. The key to transforming a diminutive bathroom into one that meets your needs and desires lies in knowing what you really want. The main issues are likely to be storage, fixtures, and surfaces. With the evolution of bathroom design, there are so many answers to common problems available in every price range that you can achieve the bathroom you want, whether you are refreshing an existing older bathroom to be pretty as well as practical or creating a small but special bathroom from scratch.

RIGHT: The clever design makes the most of this long, narrow bathroom. A double vanity contains plenty of storage and workspace. Installing a large mirror over the vanity helps to produce the feeling of having twice the space. The clear shower door seems to disappear, creating the illusion of open space.

ANOTHER SPACE-SAVING TRICK IS TO INSTALL WALL-MOUNTED FIXTURES, LEAVING MORE OPEN SURFACE AREA.

LEFT: A deep tub nestled in the alcove adds a feeling of luxury without taking up extra space.

ABOVE: This elegant console sink is perfect for a small room. Its open design creates the illusion of space. A wide surround on the sink puts toiletries within easy reach.

A B O V E : Since this bathroom is actually part of the bedroom, it presented a number of challenges when it came to defining the space and fitting in basic amenities.

The homeowners opted for a generously sized shower stall instead of a tub. The long, low cabinet makes a perfect transition between the two rooms.

LEFT, TOP: Viewed from the bedroom, the bathroom cabinet functions as an attractive architectural element. The poured concrete above-the-counter sink looks like a piece of art. The slate floor is both beautiful and practical for the bathroom. Its color ties in with the solid-surface countertop.

LEFT, BOTTOM: Adding this little shelf to a small corner creates a nice dressing table.

VINTAGE EPHEMERA CAN MAKE A CHARM-ING DISPLAY.

Space-saving Strategies

- A shower stall takes up less space than a tub
- Use a clear shower curtain, surround, or door
- Look for ways to borrow space from an adjoining room by locating the sink or storage outside the bathroom
- Build storage vertically wherever possible
- Corner fixtures are ideal for small rooms

- Consider using a pedestal or console-style sink
- Pocket doors take up less space than hinged doors
- Install mirrors to create the illusion of more space
- A monochromatic color scheme can make a space look larger

OPPOSITE: Planning ahead and looking for opportunities are vital when working in small rooms. A corner fixture can be an ideal space saver. This particular model even features shelves underneath, maximizing the vertical area beneath the sink. The corner medicine chest continues to take advantage of what would otherwise be wasted space.

ABOVE: A small bathroom doesn't mean that you're limited to built-in fixtures. This vintage-style bath uses elegant freestanding fixtures to advantage in a tight space. The key is that the footprint of each fixture is small.

OPPOSITE: The high, vaulted ceiling of this room was designed to resemble a ship's hull, creating a spacious, airy feel. Molding adds architectural interest without taking up space. The monochromatic color scheme allows for uninterrupted visual flow.

LEFT: Built-in floor-to-ceiling cabinets provide plenty of storage. It's worth carving space from a room to create this kind of ample yet discreet storage because it will prevent clutter, which tends to make a small room look even smaller.

THIS CONSOLE-STYLE SINK TAKES UP LESS ROOM THAN A BULKY VANITY.

Two or More

A shared bathroom presents space and organizational challenges all its own, including the need for extra storage and additional privacy. The more you can plan ahead, the better your bathroom will be. Consider the ages and physical conditions of all who will use the room. If you have small children and a limited budget, concentrate on fixtures and design that will grow with them. Consider incorporating concepts of "universal design," which make a bathroom accessible to all users. Plan for logical traffic patterns to optimize use. Maximize storage and consider assigning specific storage spaces to individual users. And above all, clear out the clutter!

RIGHT: This bathroom presents the ultimate in practical solutions for multiple users. Twin pedestal sinks separated by an armoire allow for privacy and plenty of storage.

THE BEST STORAGE SOLUTIONS INCORPORATE OPEN AND HIDDEN COMPARTMENTS, AND INCLUDE BOTH DRAWERS AND CABINETS.

Fixture Basics

- Standard sink height:
  34 inches (85cm)
- Shower head height:
  79 inches (2m)
- Fixtures opposite each
  other should have a
  minimum separation
  of 30 inches (75cm)
- Shower rod:
  79 inches (2m)
- Tub deck height:
  18 inches (45cm)

TWIN EXTENDING
MIRRORS ARE A
SIMPLE, PRACTICAL
CONVENIENCE.

LEFT: Installing both a tub and shower stall is a practical luxury in a shared bath.

ABOVE: This custom vanity has twin basin-style sinks. Wide separation between the sinks gives plenty of elbowroom.

LEFT: This master bath contains a separate tub and shower, a practical option if you have the space.

ABOVE: A separate nook for the toilet allows for maximum privacy in a shared bathroom.

L E F T : Space for two needn't be grand to be practical. A simple set-up like this with dual vanities and matching mirrors may be all you need to make your bathroom more functional.

YOU CAN TRANSFORM A VINTAGE TUB INTO A SHOWER-TUB COMBINATION WITH A SPECIAL SHOWER CONVERSION KIT AVAILABLE AT MANY BATH SUPPLY STORES.

ABOVE: Shared spaces can work with any design style. The custom-designed farmhouse table holds dual sinks. Open storage underneath keeps extra towels orderly. The custom-built tallboy cabinet is modeled after the cabinetry of days gone by. Details like beaded board on the walls and tub, honeycomb mosaic floor tile, and the Windsor chair give an authentic flavor to the room.

RIGHT: This well-designed space features wonderful amenities for two. Individual sinks are a real convenience during the morning grooming rush. A separate toilet compartment makes a bathroom usable for multiple occupants simultaneously.

Planning for a Shared Bathroom

- Create a plan on paper first
- Allow for logical simultaneous traffic patterns
- A two-person tub is a good option if you have small children
- Build in storage wherever possible
- Look for adjustable-height shower heads
- Grab bars are an important safety feature
- Choose non-slip surfaces for tubs and showers
- Add a built-in bench in the shower
- Create a separate toilet area
- Use tempered glass

- Temperature-limiting and pressure-balancing plumbing are musts in rooms with younger users
- Single-control faucets are easier and safer
- Install grounded electrical outlets protected by ground-fault circuit interrupters
- Use safety latches or locks on medicine chests
- A curbless shower makes entry possible for all
- For family bathrooms choose durable fixture materials

The Warmth of Wood

Wood has a natural charm and warmth all its own, and is one of the hallmarks of country style. This versatile material is a perfect backdrop for both modern and vintage bathroom design. Depending on how you use wood, it can be either elegant or casual in its effect. Darker tones and decorative moldings create a Victorian feeling, while clean-lined blond-toned wood can be thoroughly modern. With so many choices, a professional can be of real assistance in designing a bathroom in which wood has a starring role. Don't forget to use proper sealers to protect against moisture.

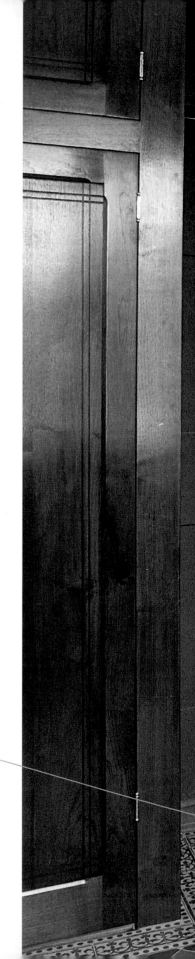

RIGHT: The rich mahogany-stained walnut and vintage-style wall and floor coverings give this bathroom the look of a nineteenth-century British men's club. Mixing patterns and colors was characteristic of the Victorian era.

THE ELABORATE TILE FLOOR MIMICS AN ORIENTAL CARPET.

OPPOSITE: Deep green tones in the woodwork complement the red hue of the walls. The lace curtain softens the overall effect.

LEFT: This modern look demonstrates that style doesn't have to cost a fortune. The stock kitchen cabinets cost less than a custom-built wood vanity. The laminate countertop looks warm but is a budget-saving option.

CEMENT-BLOCK WALL MAKES AN INTERESTING CONTRAST WITH RICH TONES OF THE WOOD. CAPPED BY WOOD MOLDING, THE CONCRETE TAKES ON A FINISHED LOOK.

RIGHT: Wood rafters, left in their natural state, give this guest bath a more intimate feel by pulling the eye down into the room. Wood touches are then drawn through the rest of the space. A room with this scale can sometimes seem cold so it's often necessary to bring in other elements to add warmth. In this case, the soft fabric of the classic toile print shower curtain does the trick. Its French country elegance immediately sets the tone for the room.

OPPOSITE: Wood elements like this country table turned dressing table and the wicker basket help extend the theme around the room.

CREATING A CUBBY UNDER A RAFTER IN OTHERWISE UNUSABLE SPACE CAN REALLY EXTEND YOUR STORAGE POSSIBILITIES.

OPPOSITE: Finishing touches above the sink include two mirrors placed one over the other. Spode transferware plates tie in perfectly with the pattern and theme of the toile shower curtain.

LEFT: The log-cabin feel of this bathroom takes full advantage of the decorative possibilities of wood. Contrasting textures like the roughhewn logs and more refined woodwork go well together because they are used consistently throughout the room. Additional natural textures, such as the Vermont granite sink surround and grasscloth vanity door-inserts, keep things interesting and make the story all about texture.

The Look for Less

- Less expensive, properly sealed wood with a deep stain looks rich and warm
- Faux finishing can offer the look of wood without the cost
- Accents like molding, beams, chair rails, corbels, or baseboards can add wood less expensively
- Choose paint or wall coverings that pick up the natural tones of the wood to enhance its warmth
- Dark wood paired with white surroundings helps ground the space

FLEA-MARKET FINDS CAN BE A GREAT WAY TO STRETCH YOUR DECORATING DOLLARS.

ABOVE: The unpainted wood doors, baseboard, and floor add a soothing natural note to this combination bathroom and sitting room. The natural cream slipcover on the chaise enhances the feeling that this is a bathroom meant for relaxation.

RIGHT: Wood furnishings can make nice finishing pieces to round out the decor of a bathroom. This antique nineteenth-century marble-topped English dressing table makes a strong statement in this otherwise plain bathroom.

Splashes of Color

Color is one of the easiest and most effective tools for changing the look and feel of a bathroom. Think about color in families—warm tones, neutrals, and cool shades—then decide on the nature of the change you want. It can perk up a tired space; turn a dull or cold room into a soothing retreat; or create a warm, cozy haven out of a forgotten corner. Among the other assets of color: it is an extremely economical way to update your bathroom; it can be used to quickly effect a transformation (and can be changed again just as easily if you feel the need); it can be used for a sweeping change or simply to introduce a fresh note.

RIGHT: The strategic mixture of lavender and blue throughout this room gives it an airy but not overpowering look. The pale grayish lavender of the walls provides just enough contrast with the crisp white tile to make the room interesting. Lavender towels and bathmat, and the blue bowl distribute the color evenly throughout the room so it looks organic.

THIS WHEELED GLASS CABINET IS A GREAT WAY TO MAKE STORAGE MORE FLEXIBLE AND PORTABLE.

The Key to This Look

The key to this two-tone look is choosing colors of similar hue and value. Hue is the color. Value is a term designers use to describe the lightness or darkness of a color. Selecting colors that are relatively close to one another creates a more soothing, restful feel than colors with a lot of contrast.

THE PRETTY, OPEN DESIGN OF THIS LATTICE SHELF PREVENTS MOISTURE BUILD-UP.

OPPOSITE: The rich shade of lavender on this marble-topped vanity makes it the focal point of the room.

LEFT: Mixing patterns, textures, and colors can make a room look busy if it is not done with care. This room does everything right. Shades of aqua, green, and lavender form a soft palette that is balanced with white. The colors are woven evenly throughout the room.

THE HAND-PAINTED DIAMOND PATTERN ON THE FLOOR CREATES INTEREST AND TIES INTO THE COLOR OF THE UPPER WALL.

RIGHT: Colored fixtures are a more permanent way to give a bathroom a distinctive look. Here, the periwinkle sinks tie in with the wall color and floor and wall tile. Silver wall sconces and medicine chest add a cool, elegant note, in keeping with the cool tones of the colors used throughout the room.

THIS WALL LEDGE IS GOOD FOR DISPLAY OR FOR FREQUENTLY USED TOILET ARTICLES.

Working with Color

- Warm colors bring life to a room
- Cool colors create a soothing environment
- Dark colors don't necessarily make a room look smaller; they make the objects in the room stand out more
- Use color consistently throughout a space
- Mixing tile colors gives a custom look to a room
- Accessories are an easy yet inexpensive way to add color

THE HAND-PAINTED TROMPE L'OEIL RUG ADDS ANOTHER PLAYFUL TOUCH.

LEFT: A small well-designed band of tile like this can be even more dramatic than a fully tile-covered wall. It's a good way to cut costs when the budget is limited.

ABOVE: The vibrant yellow plaid walls and checker-board floor give this room a sense of whimsy and fun. Striped roll-up fabric shades adorn the windows. The room works because of the overall simplicity of the color scheme and furnishings.

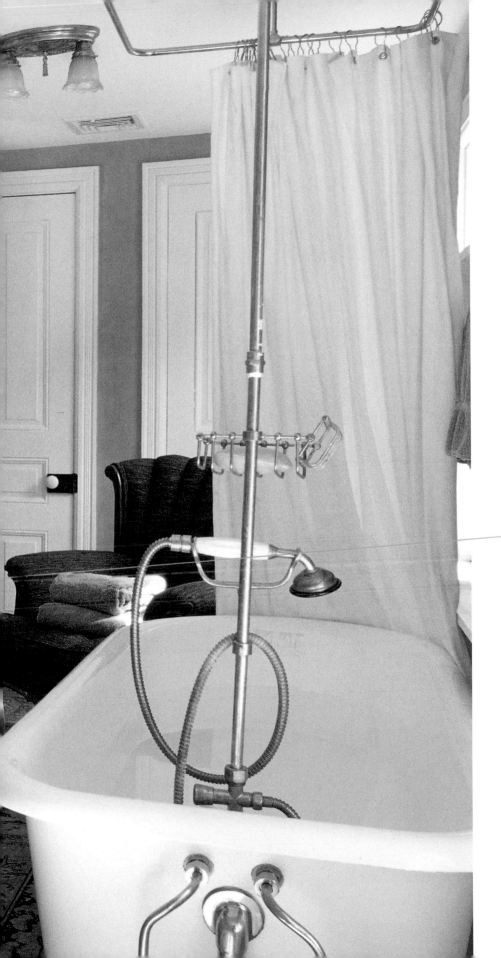

L E F T : The dramatic
approach to color gives this
room the feel of a comfortable
yet sophisticated living room,
a quality that is reinforced by
the use of an upholstered arm-
chair, oriental rugs, and hard-
wood furniture. The amethyst
towels and mauve-toned rugs
pick up all of the colors in the
chair upholstery.

THE DRY SINK ALLOWS
PLENTY OF STORAGE
SPACE FOR EVERY-
THING FROM BATH
PRODUCTS TO TREAS-
URED COLLECTIBLES.

ABOVE: Spring green makes a fresh statement in this bathroom when set against the crisp white beaded board paneling and woodwork. The shower enclosure on the left allows the clawfoot tub to take center stage. A dressing area contains both seating and storage.

RIGHT: The vintage wall-mounted sink was enclosed in a cabinet, which created extra storage space and gave the old sink new life.

Fabulous Fixtures and Handsome Hardware

The right fixtures and hardware can provide the decorative motif around which to style your dream bathroom. Hardware is the jewelry of the bathroom—but it must also be functional. Sinks, tubs, and showers are the basic elements, and come in a plethora of styles and colors. Fixtures are more versatile and give you many opportunities to experiment with different looks. Faucets and spigots that adorn the plumbing, and light fixtures that illuminate your choices are available in countless styles from reproduction Victorian to sleekly minimal.

R I G H T : This updated high-backed Victorian slipper tub allows for absolute relaxation. The unusual styling requires careful planning with regard to location of faucets and attractive views. A tub like this provides a centerpiece for the room, a focal point around which the rest of the décor is centered.

CHROME ACCENTS
REFLECT LIGHT.

ABOVE: This vintage-inspired freestanding tub has a design clean and simple enough to work in either a modern or vintage setting.

RIGHT: Antique styling and modern engineering make this faucet with handheld shower a smart choice for creating or updating a vintage bathroom.

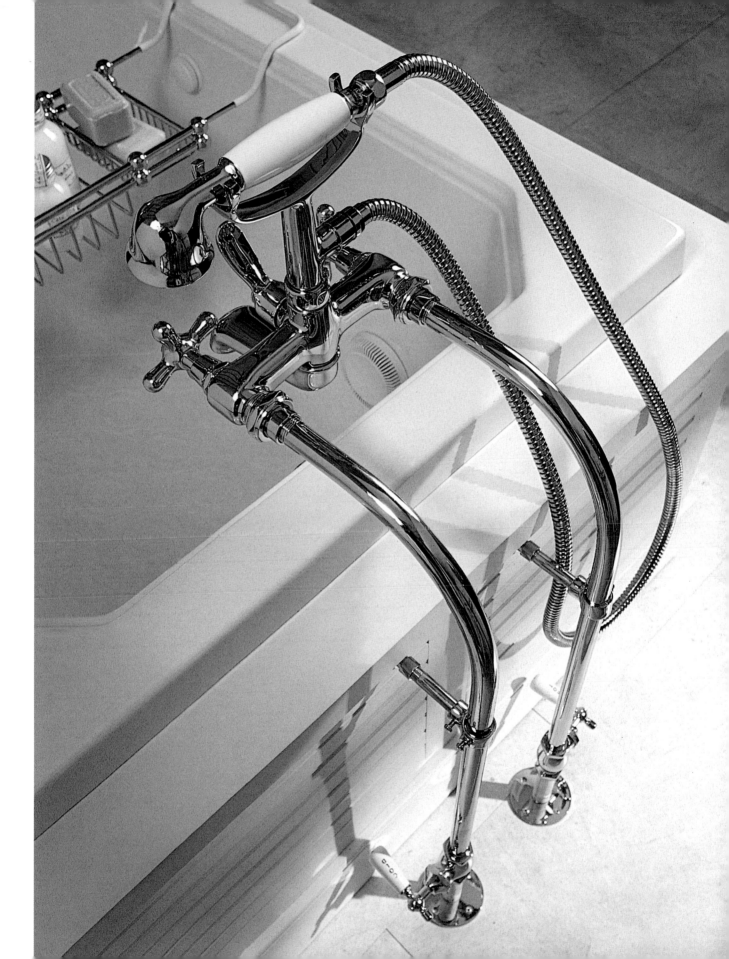

OPPOSITE: This marble-topped, wall-mounted sink came from a rummage sale. The owner had the nickel hardware stripped and lacquered. It makes a stunning focal point in the room.

LEFT, TOP: The minimalist design of this shower makes it an interesting and lighter alternative to imposing solid shower stalls. Water mists from every ring of the skeletal frame.

LEFT, BOTTOM: Building a custom shower stall is a good alternative to buying a readymade unit. The sheer size of this one makes showering a much more comfortable experience. Note how the glass walls seem to make the shower invisible.

OPPOSITE: Sinks come in so many different sizes, shapes, and colors that it may be hard to choose just one. Changing the color and style of the hardware and backgrounds gives these similarly styled sinks two completely different looks.

LEFT: Fixtures don't have to be pricey. This farmhouse table-style sink has the look of a custom fixture but not the price. The top was created from an inexpensive kitchen countertop; the twin sinks came from a thrift shop; the standard porch pillars came from a chain home improvement store. Set into an overall design that is so attractive and eye-catching, the simple hardware works; and it can always be upgraded later.

INEXPENSIVE MEDICINE CHESTS GIVE EACH PERSON STORAGE SPACE. THE SIMPLE DESIGN TIES IN TO THE CLEAN LOOK OF THE ROOM.

RIGHT: Pedestal sinks create instant style. The classic design of this one is flexible enough for either vintage or modern settings. Since they appear to take up less floor space than a vanity, pedestal sinks work as well in small rooms as they do in large rooms.

OPPOSITE, TOP: An under-mounted sink allows an interesting surface such as this old bureau to become the focal point of the sink. They do require a nice edge on the counter or vanity surface.

OPPOSITE, BOTTOM: Drop-in style sinks require no additional finishing around the edges other than caulking. The self-edging is neat and simple. They're perfect for existing vanities and less-than-perfect surfaces.

Quick Fixes for Outdated Fixtures

- Resurface them
- Repaint scratched pipes or sink legs
- Change the hardware
- Create a fabric skirt for the sink
- Enclose a built-in tub in a wood surround

LEFT: Console-style sinks can work in almost any bathroom. Since the legs are widely spaced, they are a good choice for universal access. Be sure to check the dimensions. The vintage styling of this particular sink makes it a wonderful complement to a clawfoot tub.

ABOVE: A backsplash on the sink keeps water from damaging the wall and floor around the sink. Bathroom marble should be sealed against water damage.

A B O V E : When choosing fixtures, you generally have the option of purchasing a complete suite, including tub, toilet, sink, and sometimes bidet that match or you may select pieces individually and mix and match them. A suite makes it easy to unify the look of your bath. The clean lines of this particular ensemble make it flexible enough to use in a modern, vintage, or cottage-style setting.

A B O V E : A corner shower stall like this one can fill an awkward corner without jutting awkwardly into the room. In a smaller bathroom, it's a space-saver.

A ROMAN-STYLE SHADE ALLOWS
CONTROL OF THE LIGHTING.

L E F T : Light comes from three sources in this calming room. Sconces on either side of the mirror keep the lighting balanced for grooming tasks. In addition, natural light from the over-tub window allows the bather to bask in the sun's glow.

VERSATILE BENCHES CAN BE USED FOR SEATING OR STORAGE, AND ARE PORTABLE.

OPPOSITE, TOP:
A handheld shower in the tub allows the bather to rinse off after a bath without wetting the hair. It's also good for clean-up.

OPPOSITE, BOTTOM:
Originally designed to mix water in the sink, separate "hot" and "cold" faucets give an authentic vintage look to a bathroom. They can be some-what impractical for today's more harried lifestyles. This is strictly a "grown-ups only" feature as small children can easily get burned.

LEFT: Vintage-style hard-ware fits perfectly with this sink. Hardware comes in many different finishes so be sure to explore the options before making a final choice.

Organize!

Organization is one of the main challenges in modern home design. Finding attractive and practical storage for all the items you and your family use while in bathroom—and keeping them at once accessible and out of the way—can require a lot of ingenuity. It becomes even more critical if you are a fan of today's clean, elegant styles. Luckily there are many surprisingly simple solutions available. Plan your storage approach by making a list of items you need to keep on hand, from large to small. Note how accessible they need to be—within reach, within sight, or just nearby. Then you can consider your options.

RIGHT: This bathroom contains several straight-forward storage solutions. The double vanity has multiple drawers and cupboards. A bench keeps towels within easy reach of the shower. The area under the bench works as additional storage space.

BASKETS KEEP STORAGE CLEAN, SIMPLE, AND UNCLUTTERED.

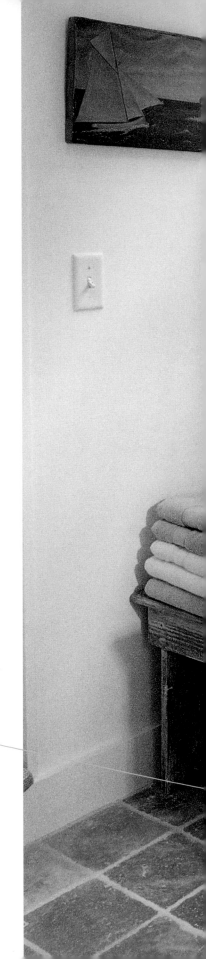

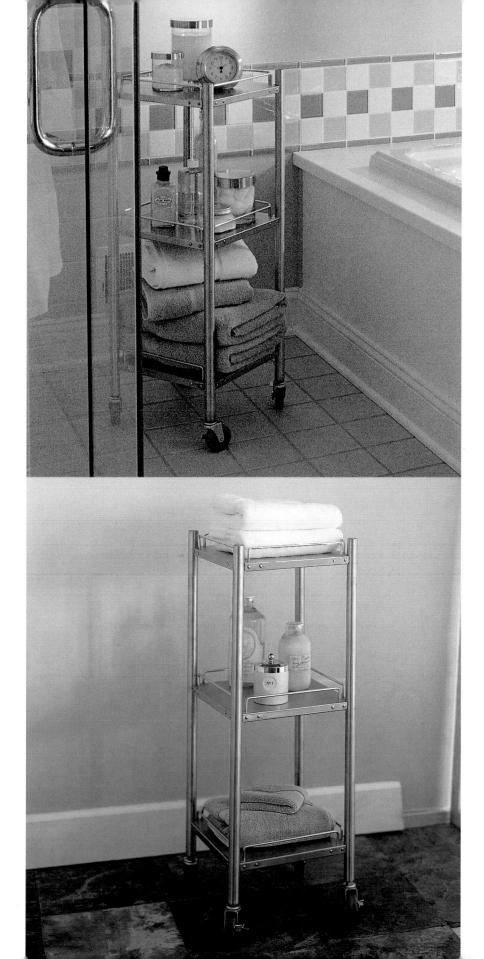

OPPOSITE: This small table is packed with big storage solutions. By transferring commonly used bath products like bath salts, soaps, and bath bombs to matching clear glass canisters, you eliminate the clutter of lots of individual packages and create an attractive unified display at the same time. Drawers allow for discreet storage and the lower shelf provides additional space for display or storage.

LEFT, TOP: A rolling cart places toiletries close at hand.

LEFT, BOTTOM: A simple, practical design allows the rolling cart to fit comfortably into any décor.

ABOVE: Storage is only one of the virtues of these unassuming drawers. In reality, they're warming drawers used in kitchens but here, they keep towels toasty warm on chilly mornings. Kitchen storage can often be adapted to bathrooms.

RIGHT: The minimalist styling of this wall-mounted shelf unit covers a lot of bases. Shelves, towel bars, and a movable mirror provide all the function of individual bulkier elements but work vertically to utilize a small band of unused space.

LEFT: This recessed medicine chest has all of the function of its less attractive predecessors but much more style. Beautiful silver molding surrounds the closed door, giving it the look of a simple, elegantly framed mirror.

ABOVE: Glass shelves create storage but place the focus on the objects resting upon them, making this type of shelving perfect for small spaces or situations where the objects themselves might be overwhelmed by the shelf. Here, clear glass is the unifying medium of all of the decorative objects.

Accessories and other Creature Comforts

Accessories are the finishing touches of any great bathroom design. They can range from the purely practical to the simply decorative, but however they are used, accessories personalize and give character to a room. Therefore, a limited budget is not a handicap because your personal style and creativity should play the biggest roles when you are choosing bathroom accessories. Keep an open mind, and don't limit yourself to obvious bathroom choices—this is a great opportunity to introduce interesting elements into your décor, from repurposed wire baskets for storage to framed vintage ephemera.

RIGHT: The vintage feel of the fixtures in this bathroom is enhanced through the use of accessories. The mirror lends a touch of faded elegance to the room. Its scale balances the chunkiness of the tub and vanity. Fabric touches like the sheer curtains, chair upholstery, and even the towels lend softness and texture.

HOOKS ARE CONVENIENT TOWEL HOLDERS, AND THEIR LOOKS ADD TO THE CHARM.

RIGHT: This small, plain hand mirror looks beautiful clustered with silver candleholders and glass bottles, all set against the gleaming white background.

OPPOSITE: This worn little vintage cabinet adds character to this room. Its distressed finish links it to the flower-filled box on the vanity.

GROUPING LIKE OBJECTS TOGETHER GIVES THEM VISUAL IMPACT.

Budget Makeover

- Change the towels, shower curtain, and bathmat
- Display towels folded on a shelf for a lush, fluffy look
- Paint is an inexpensive way to refresh a tired bathroom
- Put cotton swabs, balls, bath salts, and so on into pretty containers
- Change the mirror

THE WHITE CHERUB SCONCES ADD BAL- ANCED LIGHTING ON EITHER SIDE OF THE MIRROR. AN ORNATE DESIGN LIKE THIS WORKS WELL IN THIS SIMPLE BACKGROUND.

L E F T : Towels come in textures, colors, and prices to suit every budget and can instantly change the look and feel of a room. Switch to a new color, try a pattern or stripe, or upgrade to super-fluffy.

A B O V E : The dark frame of this mirror helps to ground the otherwise white room. Though functional items, the towels here also act as decorative objects to warm the room.

LEFT: This shower curtain has the look of a vintage chenille bedspread. Paired with the solid aqua and white towels and embroidered sheer curtains, it gives the bathroom a soft, distinctive look.

ABOVE: Don't be stuck with the idea that art is one particular thing. This unusual wall hanging is an old section of picket fence.

Finishing Touches

- Display collections—make sure they can handle the humidity
- Mix objects of different heights to create visual interest
- Look around to see what you've already got rather than rushing out to buy
- Group objects by color or theme so they have visual impact
- Just because it's not a painting doesn't mean it doesn't belong on a wall

ABOVE: This hobnail milk glass candy dish makes a perfect soap dish. Embroidered fingertip towels ground the dish and create a welcoming environment for guests.

ABOVE : A garden trellis makes a novel towel rack.
Resting on an old galvanized tub that holds sponges and
brushes, the whole thing becomes a conversation piece.

Paint and Paper

Paint is the workhorse of wall treatments. It's inexpensive, effective, simple to apply (and therefore to change), easy to care for—and most important, a coat of paint can completely transform the look and feel of a bathroom. In addition to the traditional glossy finish, you can now easily find latex flat finish paints that are washable and moisture-resistant, making them perfect for damp, high-traffic areas like the bathroom. Paint also allows you to be creative. You can experiment with color (try cool tones for an airy, spacious feeling, even in a small room, or warmer shades for a cozier feeling), take a two-tone approach, or apply stripes, faux finishes, stenciling, or trompe l'oeil effects.

Wallpaper is another way to add flair to your bathroom. Wallpapers come in special, vinyl-coated styles intended for use in bathrooms, but if your bathroom has sufficient ventilation, you may be able to use a non-coated variety. (It's best to check with a wallpaper supplier for advice.) You can use wallpaper extensively to create a patterned look, or sparingly, applying just borders.

And don't forget the ceiling in your paint or paper plans—it's as integral a part of the space as the walls or floor.

RIGHT: The distressed paint finish of the brick wall in combination with the sheer delicate curtains is an elegant counterpoint to the rawness of this loft bathroom. A similar treatment on the small cabinet ties it together.

A B O V E : Pistachio is a bold color choice that works well in this bathroom against the clean, white tile and simple fixtures. It looks fresh and invigorating, and it makes the white tile "pop."

ABOVE: A creative approach to texture and color makes this small bathroom stylish. The wainscoting was applied horizontally, for a unique look, then was given a coat of taupe paint. The subtle color, which is repeated on the window trim, emphasizes the woodwork without being overpowering, while other colors in the room are soft and muted; the overall effect is tranquil and sophisticated.

A B O V E : Paint is used subtly in this bathroom. A very dark stain grounds the floor, and is repeated on the door, then echoed in the freestanding furniture pieces. Balancing the intensity of the wood is a soft white on the beaded-board wainscoting, which emphasizes its texture. Above the wainscoting, a creamier white completes the picture.

A B O V E : Wallpaper is an excellent choice if you want to create an air of refinement. This elegant paper sports a subtle diamond pattern that adds interest to the walls without overwhelming the other elements. Note how the marble tiles are set on a diagonal to echo the wall pattern, while the mosaic tile trim features inset diamonds.

RIGHT: Sometimes when you don't have the budget to retile, the solution to refreshing dated-looking old colored tile is to add more of the color and then add a second (or third) color evenly around the room. Here, the choice of gold-and-black striped wallpaper integrates the tile beautifully. Even the black stripe now looks chic.

OPPOSITE: Wallpaper is at once a traditional and versatile choice. Although it requires more work than painting, it also allows for more ornate designs than an ordinary paint job can accommodate. In a small bathroom, it can effect a major transformation. A rope-patterned wallpaper is the star of this guest bathroom.

Creative Tilework

Decorative tile has been used throughout the world since ancient times. As a result, there is an abundance of choice, from simple white tiles to the elaborate patterns and textures that characterize various ethnic or period styles. That means that tile is a perfect medium from which to create a personal design statement, especially in the bathroom, where tile is also supremely functional. There are numerous choices in tiling materials, including ceramic, glass, and stone—again, it is always worthwhile to consult an expert before making a decision on the type of tile that is right for your bathroom. Then the fun can begin—color, texture, and pattern are all important elements of a tile design. Tile is a more permanent medium for your designs, so be sure to consider your choices thoroughly before you begin.

RIGHT: A variety of differently shaped marble tiles are used to give this bathroom a unified style that is also visually exciting. The silver-veined marble looks dramatically different in each form, from the small squares that make up the center floor to the larger tiles that frame the tub area to the rectangular tiles that form the rub surround. Marble is porous, so it should be specially sealed when used in the bathroom.

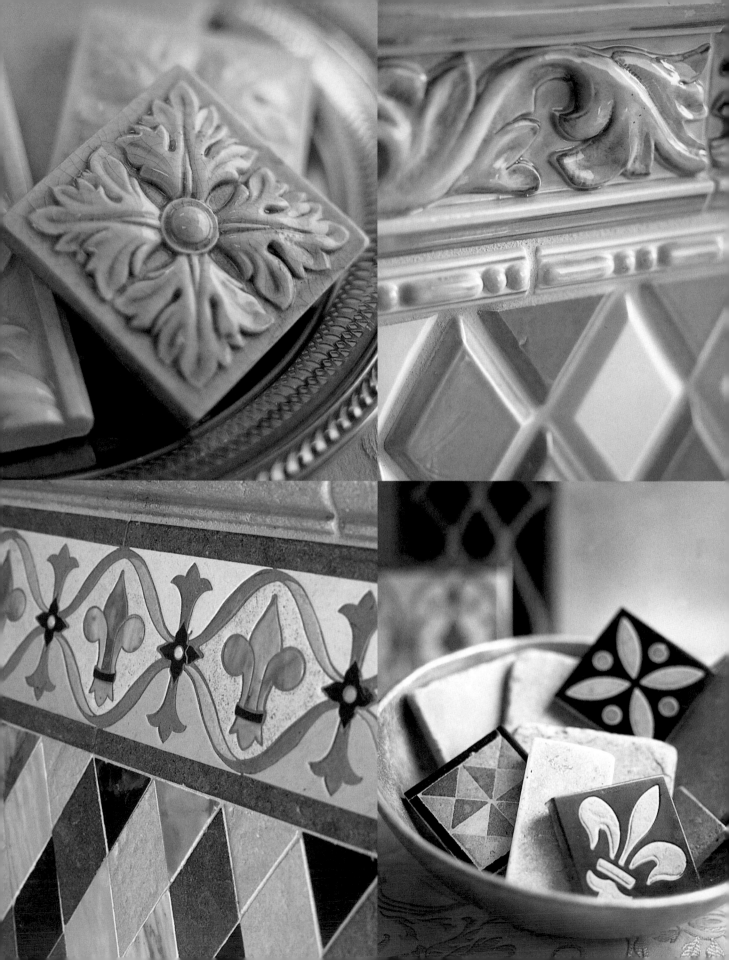

OPPOSITE : Tiles may be flat or sculptural, smooth or textured. Styles range from ultra-modern to reproductions of vintage and period looks. Using borders, mosaics, and inserts to supplement basic floor and wall tiles, you can create the designs to match almost any vision you can dream up.

ABOVE : You do not have to tile every surface, but can use border tiles to highlight elements of your décor. The tile frame surrounding this mirror echoes the ceiling border, while a more ornate design caps the lower portion of the wall. A muted color palette brings it all together.

A B O V E : The tile backdrop on this wall creates a frame for the mirror and lighting fixtures while also balancing the proportions of the sink and mirror. Otherwise, the mirror could seem lost on such a large wall. Setting the tiles diagonally makes the pattern more interesting.

ABOVE : In this temple of modernity, the three-dimensional texture of the tile on the tub surround makes a dramatic impact, breaking up the strong horizontal lines of the room. A row of sculptural tiles in a soft white adds a more organic touch above the sink.

EXTENDING THE SHELF FROM THE VANITY TO THE TUB CREATES A HANDY STORAGE AREA.

Index

Photo Credits

Country Living would like to thank the many photographers whose work appears on these pages.

Jacket
Front jacket—©David Prince; Back jacket (top left)—©Keith Scott Morton; Back jacket (top right)—©Keith Scott Morton; Back jacket (bottom)—©Keith Scott Morton; Spine—Courtesy Restoration Hardware

Page 1—Courtesy Kohler; Page 2—©Ray Kachatorian; Page 3—©Keith Scott Morton; Page 5 (top)—©Keith Scott Morton; Page 5 (middle)—©Keith Scott Morton; Page 5 (bottom)—©William P. Steele

Foreword
Page 7—©Keith Scott Morton

Introduction
Page 11—©Keith Scott Morton

White on White
Pages 12-13—©Keith Scott Morton; Page 14—©Ray Kachatorian; Page 15—©Keith Scott Morton; Page 16—©William P. Steele; Page 17—©Jim Bastardo; Page 18—©Keith Scott Morton; Page 19—©Keith Scott Morton; Page 20—©Chuck Baker; Page 21—©Keith Scott Morton

Vintage Chic
Pages 22-23—©Keith Scott Morton; Page 24—©Keith Scott Morton; Page 25—©William P. Steele; Page 26—©Keith Scott Morton; Page 27—©Keith Scott Morton; Page 28—©Bill Stern; Page 29—©William P. Steele; Pages 30-31—©Keith Scott Morton; Page 32—©Keith Scott Morton; Page 33—©Ray Kachatorian

Soothing Spaces
Pages 34-35—©Keith Scott Morton; Pages 36-37—Courtesy American Standard; Page 38—©Keith Scott Morton; Page 39—Courtesy American Standard; Page 40—©Keith Scott Morton; Page 41—©Keith Scott Morton; Page 42—©Keith Scott Morton; Page 43—©Keith Scott Morton; Page 44—©Keith Scott Morton; Page 45—©Keith Scott Morton

Small Space Solutions
Pages 46-47—©Keith Scott Morton; Page 48—©Keith Scott Morton; Page 49—Courtesy Kohler; Page 50—©Keith Scott Morton; Page 51 (top)—©Keith Scott Morton; Page 51 (bottom)—©Keith Scott Morton; Page 52—Courtesy American Standard; Page 53—Courtesy Kohler; Page 54—©Keith Scott Morton; Page 55—©Keith Scott Morton

Two or More
Pages 56-57—©Keith Scott Morton; Page 58—©Keith Scott Morton; Page 59—©Keith Scott Morton; Page 60—©Keith Scott Morton; Page 61—©Keith Scott Morton; Pages 62-63—©Keith Scott Morton; Page 64—©Keith Scott Morton; Page 65—Courtesy Kohler

The Warmth of Wood
Pages 66-67—©Keith Scott Morton; Page 68—©Keith Scott Morton; Page 69—©Keith Scott Morton; Page 70—©Keith Scott Morton; Page 71—©Keith Scott Morton; Page 72—©Keith Scott Morton; Page 73 (top)—©Keith Scott Morton; Page 73 (bottom)—©Keith Scott Morton; Page 74—©Steve Gross and Sue Daley; Page 75—©Keith Scott Morton

Splashes of Color
Pages 76-77—©; Page 78—©Keith Scott Morton; Page 79—©Keith Scott Morton; Pages 80-81—©Keith Scott Morton; Page 82—©Keith Scott Morton; Page 83—©Paul Wicheloe; Pages 84-85—©Keith Scott Morton; Page 86—©Keith Scott Morton; Page 87—©Keith Scott Morton

Fabulous Fixtures and Handsome Hardware
Pages 88-89—Courtesy Kohler; Page 90—Courtesy Kohler; Page 91—©Keith Scott Morton; Page 92—©Michael Luppino; Page 93 (top)—©Keith Scott Morton; Page 93 (bottom)—©Keith Scott Morton Page 94 (top)—©Keith Scott Morton; Page 94 (bottom)—©Keith Scott Morton; Page 95—©Michael Luppino; Page 96—Courtesy Kohler; Page 97 (top)—Courtesy American Standard; page 97 (bottom)—Courtesy American Standard; Page 98—Courtesy Restoration Hardware; Page 99—©Keith Scott Morton; Page 100—Courtesy Kohler; Page 101—Courtesy American Standard; Pages 102-103—Courtesy Kohler; Page 104 (top)—Courtesy American Standard; Page 104 (bottom)—©William P. Steele; Page 105—©William P. Steele

Organize!
Pages 106-107—©Keith Scott Morton; Page 108—Courtesy Minh & Wass; Page 109—©Keith Scott Morton; Page 110—©William P. Steele; Page 111—©William P. Steele; Page 112—©Helen Norman; Page 113 (top)—©Keith Scott Morton; Page 113 (bottom)—Courtesy Restoration Hardware; Page 114—©Keith Scott Morton; Page 115—©Keith Scott Morton; Page 116—©Keith Scott Morton; Page 117—©Keith Scott Morton

Accessories and other Creature Comforts
Pages 118-119—©Keith Scott Morton; Page 120—©Keith Scott Morton; 121—©Keith Scott Morton; Page 122—©Steven Randazzo; Page 123—©Steve Gross and Sue Daley; Page 124—©Jessie Walker; Page 125—©Jessie Walker; Page 126—©Andrew McCaul; Page 127—©Sean Sullivan

Paint and Paper
Pages 128-129—©Keith Scott Morton; Page 130—Courtesy American Standard; Page 131—©William P. Steele; Page 132—Courtesy Kohler; Page 133—Courtesy Walker Zanger; Page 134—©Steven Randazzo; Page 135—©Keith Scott Morton

Creative Tilework
Pages 136-137—Courtesy Walker Zanger; Page 138 (top left)—Courtesy Walker Zanger; Page 138 (top right)—Courtesy Walker Zanger; Page 138 (bottom right)—Courtesy Walker Zanger; Page (bottom left)—Courtesy Walker Zanger; Page 139—Courtesy Walker Zanger; Page 140—Courtesy Walker Zanger; Page 141—Courtesy Walker Zanger